Rwanda

An

Agenda for

International Action

Guy Vassall-Adams

Oxfam Publications

A catalogue record for this book is available from the British Library

ISBN 0 85598 299 3

Published by Oxfam (UK and Ireland)
274 Banbury Road, Oxford OX2 7DZ, UK
(registered as a charity, no. 202918)

Available in Ireland from: Oxfam in Ireland, 19 Clanwilliam Terrace,
Dublin 2; tel. 01 661 8544.

Co-published in Australia by Community Aid Abroad, and available
from them at 156 George Street, Fitzroy, Victoria 3065, Australia
(tel.+61 3 289 9444; fax +61 3 419 5318/5895).

Community Aid Abroad are co-publishing this book, and invite
readers to consider its conclusions, as a contribution to discussion and
debate on events in Rwanda and their implications for international
peace and development.

Designed and typeset by Oxfam Design , OX1340/MJ/PK/94
Printed by Oxfam Print Unit
on environment-friendly paper
Set in 10/12.5 point Palatino with Franklin Gothic Book and Demi

Contents

Foreword

The campaign of genocide and the refugee crises which have devastated Rwanda since April 1994 have stunned the world. They prompted Oxfam (UK and Ireland) to undertake one of the largest emergency operations in its 50-year history. They have also prompted the most generous response from the British and Irish public that Oxfam has ever been privileged to witness.

We are all responsible for ensuring that suffering on such a vast scale never happens again. But if Rwanda is to have any hope of recovering from the catastrophe which befell it in 1994, the world community must attempt to understand what made that catastrophe possible.

The tragedy of Rwanda has demonstrated more clearly than ever before that the international community lacks the capacity to respond effectively to such crises. The political will to act is in very short supply; and radical reforms need to be undertaken if the world is to be ready to take effective action. This book attempts to shed light on the initiatives that could help Rwanda to recover, and the reforms that could prevent another such disaster, in Rwanda or elsewhere.

In Part One, events in 1994 are situated in the context of Rwanda's history, and that of Burundi. Because Burundi's political history since Independence has been almost a mirror image of Rwanda's, events in one country have had a major impact upon events in the other. This is true of the recent past, when the October 1993 coup in Burundi, dashing hopes of Hutu majority rule, played directly into the hands of President Habyarimana in Rwanda, as he sought to stall power-sharing with his opponents, the Rwandese Patriotic Front. It is also likely to be true for the future.

But an understanding of the regional refugee situation before April 1994 is also essential to an assessment of the challenges which confront Rwanda. The history of the Rwandese diaspora illustrates many of the issues which Rwanda and the Great Lakes Region now face in a much starker form, following the refugee crises of 1994. If the world is to assist the region in its efforts to meet these challenges, it must understand the issues raised by the presence of nearly two million Rwandese people living in neighbouring countries.

Part Two of the book deals with the political developments and human rights abuses which preceded the campaign of genocide. It shows that, far from being ignorant of what was going on, the international community was well aware of the situation in Rwanda, but that there was insufficient political will to face up to its implications. Hence the continuing arms supplies to the Rwandese government, and the desire of member states to reduce the size of the UN's presence.

Part Three describes the campaign of genocide and the refugee crises, and the international community's response to both. It describes the failure of UN member states to protect civilians from genocide, and the international response to the refugee crisis in Goma.

Part Four draws conclusions from this account, and makes detailed recommendations to the government of Rwanda, the regional powers, and the wider international community. The challenge is for governments to demonstrate that an 'international community' actually exists, by mustering the political will to act in the name of common humanity.

David Bryer
Director
Oxfam (UK and Ireland)
September 1994

3

Summary

When the Hutu ethnic majority gained power in Rwanda following Independence from colonial rule in 1962, they over-turned centuries of political and economic dominance by the minority Tutsi. But tensions fostered by Rwanda's colonial experience found expression in rising levels of violence, which prompted thousands of Tutsi to flee to neighbouring countries.

The question of the refugees' right to return began to dominate Rwanda's political agenda when a rebel army representing the refugees (the Rwandese Patriotic Front — RPF) invaded Rwanda in 1990. The international community sponsored a 'peace process' which aimed to bring about power-sharing.

But in 1991 and 1992 there was increasing evidence that the Rwandese government was violating with impunity the human rights of its political opponents and of ordinary Tutsi citizens. At the same time, some Northern governments continued to arm President Habyarimana's military forces. In August 1993, a peace accord was signed, with the backing of the international community, and UN forces were sent to Rwanda. But the warning signs were largely ignored, as UN member states tried to reduce the size of the UN force, in order to save money.

In April 1994 the President of Rwanda was assassinated, and Hutu extremists embarked on a campaign of genocide in an attempt to eliminate their political opponents. The United Nations Security Council abandoned the Rwandese people to their terrible fate by withdrawing most of the UN force, and failing to send a new contingent to protect civilians under threat.

As the killings escalated, the RPF advanced across Rwanda, and during July established control over the country. By then, how-ever, genocide had claimed an estimated one million lives, and much of Rwanda had been depopulated by the catastrophic exodus of refugees into Tanzania and Burundi.

During July 1994, a refugee crisis of even greater dimensions developed, when nearly one million Hutu fled to Goma in Zaire. The international response was far less effective than it might have been, had there been better planning, preparation, consultation, and co-ordination. Thousands of Rwandese lives were needlessly lost.

Rwanda now faces the huge challenges of reconstruction and rehabilitation, and the task of forging a political solution that will secure a peaceful future for all its citizens. A real and lasting commitment to these tasks is vital, not only from the new government of Rwanda, but also from regional powers and the wider international community. And if such tragedies are to be prevented from happening again, the UN will have to be given the means to respond effectively.

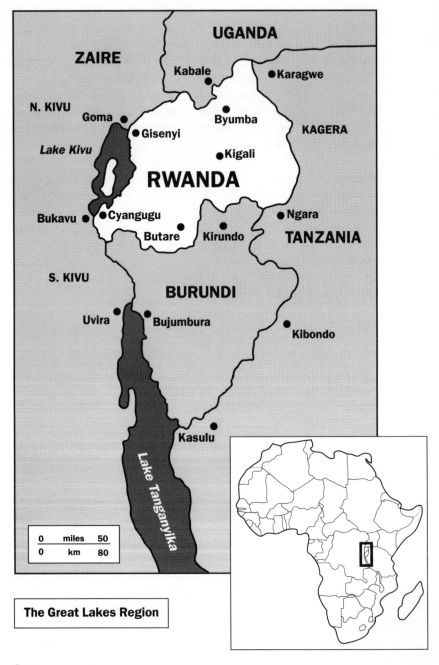

The Great Lakes Region

Rwanda and Burundi before Independence

Four hundred years ago, a group of people called Tutsi established feudal kingdoms in the lands now called Rwanda and Burundi. They formed a land-owning and cattle-owning aristocracy, ruling over the Hutu, a larger group, who were farmers. In return for their labour, Hutu were granted the use of land and cattle, and the protection of their overlords. The Twa, who lived as hunter-gatherers, made up a tiny fraction of the population and lived a marginal existence.

Tutsi controlled the three main sources of power: the cattle economy, the monarchy, and religious life. Their rule was reinforced by an oral mythology which taught that Tutsi were inherently superior and that their dominance was ordained by God. The Tutsi *mwami* (king) stood at the apex of this complex social order, which encompassed three different sets of chieftaincies over land, cattle, and the military. But despite the hierarchical nature of this society, it was unusually unified. Tutsi and Hutu lived together, shared the same language (Kinyarwanda) and, in most important respects, the same culture.

The colonial era: Tutsi dominance endorsed

The German colonialists who first encountered this way of life in the 1890s identified with the Tutsi and pronounced them to be an elite of nilo-hamitic origin. This racialist theory, widely challenged today, became the ideological justification for the colonialists' decision to govern Rwanda and Burundi through indirect rule, via the Tutsi monarchy. In practical terms, indirect rule was opportunistic, because it required few German administrators and was therefore very cheap. The Germans administered Rwanda and Burundi as a single state, Rwanda-Urundi.

The imposition of indirect rule changed the character of the system of patronage and protection. The feudal system, exploitative as it was, had none the less established reciprocal obligations and allowed for a degree of social mobility. The ruling class had clear responsibilities towards their underlings, and Hutu could rise to the status of Tutsi by acquiring wealth, in the form of cattle.

Indirect rule, under first the Germans and then the Belgians, who took over Rwanda and Burundi at the end of the First World War, destroyed the checks and balances of the feudal system and deprived Hutu of all their social entitlements. The Germans began this process by replacing Rwanda's only Hutu chiefs, in the north-west, with Tutsi chiefs. This prompted a short-lived popular uprising in 1910, which was swiftly crushed by colonial military forces.

The Belgians introduced forced labour, appointing Tutsi administrators to supervise Hutu labourers, who were now compelled to work for nothing in return. During the 1930s the Belgians conducted a census which declared the Tutsi to form 14 per cent of the population and the Hutu 85 per cent; however, they decided to classify any individual with fewer than ten cows as a Hutu. Identity cards were introduced, specifying the ethnic group of the owner.

People classified as Tutsi were systematically favoured in the education system and the colonial administration. Hutu were largely denied access to education, with the major exception of training for the Catholic priesthood. The majority were, in effect, assigned the status of a permanent underclass, excluded from the power structures of their country.

After the Second World War, Rwanda-Urundi became a Trustee Territory of the United Nations. During the 1950s, the United Nations put pressure on the Belgian authorities to grant the country independence and introduce elected advisory structures. The Belgians were already beginning to support Hutu aspirations for a greater role in their country's affairs, believing that minority rule was unsustainable, and fearful of the pan-Africanist tendencies which they discerned among the Tutsi ruling class. Now, developments in what were to become separate countries — Rwanda and Burundi — began to diverge.

The end of colonialism: power shifts to the Hutu

In Rwanda, the Belgians began to replace Tutsi chiefs with Hutu chiefs, and actively encouraged the nascent Hutu opposition. But the Tutsi were loath to accept that the days of minority rule were over, while the Hutu aggressively asserted their new-found power. The run-up to Rwanda's first local elections in 1960 was marred by violent conflict between supporters of the new Hutu party, the Party of the Movement for Hutu Emancipation (PARMEHUTU), and supporters of the pro-Tutsi party, the National Rwandese Union (UNAR). Several hundred people were killed and some 220,000 were internally displaced.

Many of the new Hutu mayors who came to power in 1960 used their positions to persecute Tutsi, thousands of whom were forced to abandon their homes and flee abroad. Their flight initiated a new pattern of violence. Tutsi refugees in neighbouring countries (Uganda, Burundi, Zaire, and Tanzania) organised themselves into militias, in the hope of returning by force and restoring Tutsi rule. But their attacks upon Hutu officials in Rwanda provoked retaliatory killings of Tutsi civilians still living in the country.

The violence unleashed in the run-up to Independence continued during the 1960s. Tutsi refugees, referred to as the *Inyenzi* (cockroaches), made repeated attempts to restore Tutsi rule by launching military attacks from abroad. In December 1963, Tutsi refugees launched an attack from Burundi, after which 10,000 Tutsi were massacred by Hutu gangs. Every attack and the subsequent reprisals created new waves of refugees; by 1964 the United Nations High Commissioner for Refugees (UNHCR) estimated that over 150,000 Rwandese had fled to surrounding countries.

The refugees abandoned their raids in 1967, despairing of restoring Tutsi rule. But many did not abandon their hopes of one day returning to their homeland. Rwanda's Hutu-dominated governments, however, feared that permitting the refugees to return would jeopardise their newly-won power. General Juvenal Habyarimana, who came to power in a military coup in 1973, argued that their return was simply impossible. Population pressure was already too great, he argued; there was already too little land, too few jobs, and too little food.

Under international law, refugees have the right to return to their country of origin, but for the following fifteen years Habyarimana would consider only individual applications for repatriation. One of the conditions he laid down was that applicants had to be able to support themselves after their return. The result was that only a handful of refugees returned each year; for 1986 the figure is believed to have been 14. The refugees, however, continued to assert their 'right to return', regardless of wealth.

Rwanda since Independence

Rwanda had become independent on 1 July 1962. Hutu majority rule, which was to last for more than thirty years, had finally begun. During this time Rwanda made significant progress towards developing its economic potential; between 1965 and 1980, Rwanda's Gross National Product per capita grew by an annual rate of 1.6 per cent.[1] The combination of a generally well-managed economy and pragmatic development policies resulted in an influx of aid from Northern donors. Together these transformed the road network, gave clean water to 70 per cent of Rwandese, created a peasants' bank, and established the best-trained civil service in the region.

The hunger for land

But for ordinary Rwandese, daily life continued to be a remorseless struggle for survival. Over 90 per cent of Rwandese worked as subsistence farmers, growing their own crops on small plots of land. But with 7.2 million people in a country about the same size as Belgium, Rwanda had the highest population density in Africa. With a rapidly growing population, the shortage of land became ever more acute. Between 1966 and 1983, Rwanda achieved impressive increases in food production — an annual average increase of 4.3 per cent — mostly by bringing marginal lands into cultivation. But between 1984 and 1989 food production increased by only one per cent per annum,[2] as the supply of new land began to run out. Rwanda was finding it increasingly difficult to feed itself.

Rwanda's economic development was inhibited by its lack of natural resources, and its landlocked location, 1,500 km from the nearest sea-port at Mombasa in Kenya. Rwanda's internal market was tiny, but the country had little to export to the outside world. Its major export crops were coffee and tea, accounting for over 80 per cent of exports in 1992. This high degree of dependence on the

11

two commodities made the country extremely vulnerable to fluctuations in their world market prices. When the International Coffee Agreement collapsed in 1987, the price of Rwandese coffee fell to half its 1980 level. The government was forced to cut the price paid to producers, and to devalue the Rwandese Franc by 67 per cent. This had a major impact on the living standards of producers, on the economy generally, and on social welfare provision, as the government was forced by declining revenues to cut back its expenditure.

On the margins of survival

Central and local government were Rwanda's largest employers, giving work to 7,000 people in the former sector and 43,000 in the latter during the 1980s. But with many thousands of young people joining the job market each year, the disparity between opportunity and demand was huge. In a country without social security, to be unemployed is to exist on the very margins of survival; most Rwandese could not expect to live more than 46 years. Ever since Independence, thousands of Rwandese have left their country every year in a desperate search for opportunities in neighbouring countries.

The lack of opportunities was exemplified by the education system. Only six per cent of Rwandese went to secondary school; less than one per cent to university. As employment opportunities dwindled during the 1980s, even the highly qualified minority could not be sure of a job. Taken as a whole, the 1980s saw a dramatic decline in Rwanda's economic fortunes: between 1980 and 1991, GNP per capita fell by an annual rate of 2.4 per cent,[3] and the nation's total debt stocks jumped from US$189 million to US$844 million.[4] In the late 1980s, Rwanda's economy worsened in every key area: growth rates, indebtedness, balance of payments, and terms of trade. According to the UN's Human Development Index, which takes into account life-expectancy, educational attainment, and standard of living, Rwanda was among the world's poorest countries in 1992: 153 out of 173 on the poverty scale.[5]

The Structural Adjustment Programme introduced at the behest of the World Bank in 1990 coincided with the start of a civil war initiated by the invasion of a rebel army, the Rwandese Patriotic Front (RPF). The programme was in place for a very short period of time, so it is hard to assess its overall impact. There is evidence, however, that the introduction of higher fees for health and education ('cost-sharing') added to the burdens of the poor.

The war had a devastating effect on Rwanda's economy. First, it displaced hundreds of thousands of ordinary farmers in the north, which had a dramatic impact on coffee and food production. Secondly, it cut the road to Mombasa, Rwanda's main land route to the outside world. Thirdly, it destroyed Rwanda's fledgling tourist industry, which had been the nation's third-biggest earner of foreign exchange. Finally, it prompted the President, General Habyarimana, to increase the size of the armed forces dramatically, consuming precious resources that were desperately needed for health care and education.

The Rwandese diaspora

The refugee situation in the Great Lakes Region is complicated by the fact that, before the immense refugee crises which have depopulated much of Rwanda since April 1994, there were already three distinct groups of people who originated from Rwanda but lived in neighbouring countries. Together they numbered some two million people. They are often referred to as Banyarwanda, which means they are speakers of Kinyarwanda, Rwanda's native language. In addition to these two million, about 500,000 were officially recognised as refugees, with the legal right to return to Rwanda.[6]

The first group of Banyarwanda found themselves outside Rwanda when the colonial powers determined its boundaries with Uganda and Zaire in 1910. They are now Ugandans or Zaireans who speak Kinyarwanda. Although they are ethnically classed as Banyarwanda, until an agreement in 1991 (see section below on the Dar es Salaam Declaration) they had no legal right to return to Rwanda. Both Hutu and Tutsi, they are believed originally to have numbered about half a million people in Zaire and 200,000 in Uganda.

The second group of Banyarwanda in neighbouring countries are economic migrants. In the early years of the twentieth century they left Rwanda to work on the plantations in Uganda and Zaire. More recently, many Rwandese left in search of land, joining relatives who had already established themselves. There are believed to be several hundred thousand such people in Uganda, Zaire, and Tanzania. Most of the economic migrants were Hutu.

The third group of Banyarwanda living in neighbouring countries are Tutsi refugees who left as a result of the post-Independence violence. Most of these people fled to Uganda, and until 1994 they were believed to number some 200,000 people. The

UNHCR, however, registered 80,000 as refugees in 1991, because many were self-settled.

Uganda

In Uganda, two separate developments during the 1980s dramatically heightened the need to resolve the issue of the refugees' 'right to return'. In 1982 and 1983, 80,000 Banyarwanda living throughout Uganda were driven from their land and homes by local police and militias, under the direction of politicians and local officials. Many of these people were from the first group of indigenous Banyarwanda described above. They had been born in Uganda, had lived there for the whole of their lives, and now found themselves being treated as enemies.

This violence had a profound effect upon the outlook of all Banyarwanda living in neighbouring countries. The conclusion they drew from the violence in Uganda was that, no matter how well-established they became in other countries, they would never be free from the threat of violence. Rather than continuing to be scapegoats for other countries' domestic ills, they asserted with renewed vigour and determination their right to return to Rwanda.[7]

President Habyarimana's policy on this issue changed during the 1980s. Many of the second-generation Banyarwanda in Uganda had joined Yoweri Museveni's National Resistance Army in its bid to oust President Milton Obote from power. These young, well-educated Tutsi had thereby acquired military expertise, and Habyarimana realised that, unless he began to address their demands, they might try to fight their way home.

In 1988, therefore, Habyarimana began talks with the Ugandan government on the refugees 'right to return'. During the following two years, the talks made progress on technical issues, but Habyarimana appeared unwilling to accede to the refugees' demands for political reforms that would assure them a sufficient share of civil and military power to protect their interests.

Tanzania

Until the refugee crises of 1994, most of the Rwandese refugees in Tanzania were Tutsi who had fled from Rwanda since Independence. Initially they became established at a camp at Muyenzi in the Ngara district, and later at a camp at Mwesi, farther south. Until April 1994, there were believed to be around 50,000 such people in Tanzania. In addition there was a large number of mainly Hutu people who had migrated illegally to the Kagera region of north-west Tanzania in search of land.

The refugees benefited from the relative peace and stability in Tanzania, and from the Tanzanian government's willingness to meet its obligations towards refugees under international law. The refugees were initially reluctant to become settled, fearing that to do so would be to surrender their right to return to Rwanda. But the Tanzanian authorities were anxious to see the refugees settled and self-sufficient.

In 1978 they decided to offer mass naturalisation to refugees wishing to take Tanzanian nationality. Many took up this offer, but its implementation proceeded slowly, and by the late 1980s many had still not received their naturalisation certificates. Those who did become naturalised citizens, however, appear to have become fully integrated into the life of their new country and to have been treated the same as other Tanzanian nationals in every respect.[8]

In 1990 the governments of Rwanda and Tanzania signed an accord under which illegal migrants who had entered Tanzania before 1985 would be naturalised, but those who had arrived more recently, about 30,000, would be returned to Rwanda.

Zaire

Until 1994, Zaire was host to members of all three groups of Banyarwanda refugees described above: indigenous Banyarwanda, economic migrants, and recent refugees. In parts of Kivu province, Banyarwanda outnumbered the ethnic groups who considered themselves 'true Zaireans' by four to one. They had a reputation for hard work and enterprise; some built up extremely successful businesses and acquired large areas of land, on which they raised cattle.

Partly because of this success, their status as citizens was a matter of contention. Since the 1960s a series of laws had awarded Zairean nationality to these groups, and then withdrawn it. In 1990, the authorities established a programme to identify foreigners, but it was suspended after violent protests. Elections were twice annulled in Kivu, because the 'true Zaireans' feared the loss of political power to Banyarwanda.

In March 1993 several Banyarwanda were killed by Zaireans, prompting retaliations and escalating violence over the following months which cost an estimated 6,000 lives and left about 220,000 people displaced from their homes. Dozens of villages were totally destroyed, livestock was looted, and crops were burnt.

Burundi

Before April 1994, the vast majority of Rwandese refugees in Burundi were Tutsi who had left Rwanda since Independence. Their number was recently estimated at about 250,000. A large number of these refugees had settled in Bujumbura, Burundi's capital, and established themselves as teachers, entrepreneurs, and white-collar workers. This success in part reflected the favourable political climate for Tutsi in Burundi.

Burundi since Independence

In Burundi, the Tutsi, who are in the minority, have dominated political life since Independence. Burundi's first political party, the Union for National Progress (UPRONA), formed in the run-up to Independence, was led by Prince Louis Rwagasore, a Tutsi who enjoyed the support of both ethnic groups. It won a comfortable victory in legislative and local elections held in 1961. However, in October of that year the prince was assassinated. Thereafter, political rivalries increasingly found expression in ethnic tensions and violence.

The Hutu–Tutsi power struggle in reverse

Legislative elections in 1965 gave Hutu the majority of seats in the national assembly, but the king appointed a Tutsi as Prime Minister and began to replace elected local officials with his own supporters. This prompted a coup attempt by Hutu army officers and a mutiny by Hutu soldiers. The Tutsi-dominated army crushed the revolt with extreme severity: most of Burundi's Hutu politicians, police, and army officers were killed. In 1966, Michel Micombero, a Tutsi army officer, formed a military government and declared Burundi a republic.

For the following 26 years Burundi was ruled by a succession of Tutsi-controlled military governments, backed by the Tutsi-dominated army, and willing to crush Hutu opposition with the ruthless use of force. As in Rwanda, the government's policies created hundreds of thousands of refugees (this time Hutu) and, as in Rwanda, some of these refugees launched military attacks from neighbouring countries, prompting retaliatory attacks upon (Hutu) civilians by the army.[9]

The most notorious episode took place in 1972, when Burundese Hutu from the refugee community in Tanzania launched an attack on Tutsi families in Burundi, killing up to 2,000. The army responded with a retaliation of genocidal proportions. Between 80,000 and 300,000 Hutu were killed, while hundreds of thousands fled from the country. Attacks by Hutu insurgents and violent reprisals by Burundi's army also took place in 1988 and 1991. In 1991, however, President Pierre Buyoya embarked on a series of dramatic political reforms. Power-sharing began in earnest, and presidential elections were announced for June 1993.

The presidential elections in 1993 resulted in victory for the opposition Front for Democracy in Burundi (FRODEBU), led by Melchior Ndadaye, a young Hutu banker. With 65 per cent of the vote, Ndadaye had decisively defeated President Buyoya.His victory was reinforced in the legislative elections, held several weeks later, in which FRODEBU candidates received 71 per cent of votes cast. Ndadaye did his best to allay Tutsi fears, installing a government of national unity with a Tutsi Prime Minister and nine Tutsi among the 23 ministers. However, on 21 October 1993 elements within the army launched a coup, killing President Ndadaye and briefly re-imposing military rule. The coup was immediately condemned by Northern and African governments, and foreign donor nations began announcing the withdrawal of development assistance to Burundi. Although a civilian government was soon re-appointed, the coup had rekindled violent conflict.

Hutu had taken revenge against Tutsi civilians, prompting the army and police to retaliate. The violence is estimated to have cost between 50,000 and 200,000 lives, from both ethnic groups. It also prompted 700,000 mainly Hutu refugees to flee to neighbouring countries, with the majority seeking refuge in southern Rwanda. Some 250,000 people were displaced within Burundi itself.

The October 1993 coup dealt a devastating blow to the hopes of ordinary Burundese, who had been enjoying the prospect of peaceful majority rule for the first time in their history. It also ended the repatriation of Burundese refugees from Tanzania, which had been proceeding since 1991, on the basis of an agreement between the two countries.

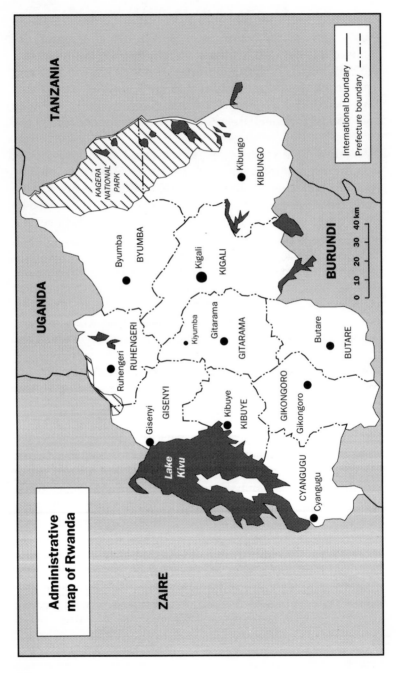

Administrative map of Rwanda

1990: the first RPF invasion

Following the end of the Cold War, Northern governments began to declare their reluctance to support African governments which failed to meet their insistence on 'good governance'. In July 1990 President Habyarimana responded to international and domestic political pressures by announcing the imminent introduction of multi-party politics. He had dismissed the suggestion only months before.[10]

In October 1990, however, 4,000 Rwandese deserters from Museveni's army entered northern Rwanda from Uganda. Most of these young fighters were Tutsi refugees, but they also included a number of prominent Hutu opponents of Habyarimana. Calling themselves the Rwandese Patriotic Front, they accused the Habyarimana regime of corruption, and demanded 'democracy'. Their tactic was to use military means to increase pressure on the government to accede to their demands for power-sharing.

Unlike the Tutsi militias of the 1960s, the RPF expressly stated that its aim was not to re-impose Tutsi hegemony. This claim was disbelieved by most of Rwanda's Hutu majority, despite considerable sympathy among southern Rwandese with the RPF's political analysis.

On first entering Rwanda, the RPF attempted to drive directly to Kigali. Within days Kigali was in panic, but once the government received the support of French and Belgian troops (brought in to 'protect their nationals') and Zairean troops, they managed to turn the tide. By the end of October the RPF appeared defeated, driven back into Uganda without its original leaders, who had been killed.

In fact, the scattered remnants of the RPF regrouped and worked their way through southern Uganda to the volcanoes that form the border with Rwanda. From this isolated base, allegedly supported by the Ugandan military, the RPF demonstrated their continued effectiveness with a spectacular attack on Ruhengeri, in which they took the prison and released all its prisoners.

The Dar es Salaam Declaration

The RPF's military gains, combined with pressure from regional powers and Northern governments, succeeded in persuading President Habyarimana to enter discussions to address the refugee question. These talks involved the Presidents of Zaire, Tanzania, Burundi, and Uganda, the Organisation of African Unity (OAU), and the UNHCR. The result was the 1991 Dar es Salaam Declaration, which gave Rwandese refugees the choice between returning to Rwanda, opting for Rwandese nationality but remaining in their host countries, and becoming nationals of their host countries, subject to the laws and policies of these governments.

For his part, General Habyarimana committed the government of Rwanda to 'finding a definitive and durable solution' to the refugee problem; acknowledged the 'legitimate right' of refugees to return; and gave his government's undertaking, 'within the spirit of its policy of political opening towards all political groupings, to remove all obstacles which impede the return of Rwandese refugees to their country and to guarantee their full participation in the democratic political process of the country'.[11]

The changing political climate

Until the invasion of the RPF in 1990, the main political issue within Rwanda had been the north/south divide. Since coming to power in 1973, President Habyarimana had consistently favoured his home region of the north-west. The north received a disproportionate share of resources, and northerners enjoyed better educational opportunities and were over-represented in government and state companies. The leading advocates of change within Rwanda were Hutu from the south, who felt they were entitled to a greater share of the country's resources.

During 1991 and 1992 there was a gradual opening up of political life within Rwanda. President Habyarimana's MRND (Movement for Reconstruction and Development) still held a monopoly on political power. But new opposition parties began to spring up, including the Social Democrats, the Liberal Party, and the Movement of Democratic Republicans (MDR), which articulated the concerns of southern Hutu, drawing support from the old PARMEHUTU constituency. It represented the main political threat to the ruling party.

Following the RPF's invasion, however, the political climate underwent a significant change. Suddenly, Tutsi found themselves being accused of collaboration with the RPF, simply because they were Tutsi. Hutu from the south, perceived as having closer links to Tutsi and as opponents of the government, also began to be branded as 'the enemy within'. It was at this stage that President Habyarimana helped to establish a new party, the Coalition for the Defence of the Republic (CDR), which advocated a policy of Hutu supremacy.

In practical terms, the RPF's invasion prompted Habyarimana to increase the size of the Rwandese army very significantly. Before October 1990 the army had comprised about 5,000 men; but by the end of October 1991 it had risen to 24,000, and would continue to rise to over 30,000 during 1992. At the same time, frequent violations of human rights were occurring — indiscriminately in the case of Tutsi citizens, more selectively in the case of political opponents of Habyarimana's government, both Hutu and Tutsi.

In addition to increasing the size of the army, the government also encouraged the formation of militias allied to the ruling MRND party and to the extremist CDR party. The militia allied to the MRND was called the *Interahamwe* ('Those who attack together'); the militia allied to the CDR was known as the *Impuzamugambi*

('Those with a single purpose'). Young men, many of whom had no work and no prospect of work, were easily recruited with promises of land, jobs, and the material rewards to be reaped from their plunder. Rwanda's poverty, and political violence, again appeared to be intimately linked.

International support

At the international level, however, Habyarimana continued to attend discussions in Arusha in Tanzania which sought to build upon the Dar es Salaam Declaration and to resolve the refugee question once and for all. The OAU again played a leading role, and the negotiations were also supported by Rwanda's neighbours and by four Northern observer countries: France, Belgium, the United States, and Germany. The main focus of the discussions was the political reforms which Habyarimana had to concede in order to persuade the RPF to honour the agreed ceasefire, and to persuade Rwandese refugees that they could return to their homeland in safety.

Both the OAU and the United Nations undertook initiatives to support the Arusha process. The OAU organised a Neutral Military Observer Group (NMOG), which arrived in the buffer zones separating RPF and government-held territories in July 1992, with a mandate to assess if and when the agreed ceasefire was violated. These 50 observers were later replaced by a larger group (NMOG II), consisting of 132 observers from OAU countries, which was given the same mandate.

United Nations support took the form of the Observer Mission Uganda–Rwanda (UNOMUR), established by Resolution 846 in June 1993, which would consist of 81 observers located in Uganda, with a mandate to assess whether the Ugandan army was supporting the RPF. This Resolution was sponsored by the French; a request by the RPF to assess whether the French were supporting the Rwandese government was turned down.

Abuses of human rights

While the talks continued at Arusha, there was growing international awareness of the human rights abuses perpetrated by Habyarimana's regime against Tutsi. In February and May 1992 the human rights non-governmental organisations (NGOs) Africa Watch[12] and Amnesty International drew attention to violations committed by the regime since 1990. Amnesty noted the extrajudicial execution of more than 1,000 Tutsi, the use of torture against detainees, 'dozens of disappearances', and the imprisonment, without charge or trial, of more than 8,000 people.[13]

Although the government subsequently released nearly all of the detainees, no one was prosecuted for these abuses, and in March 1993 an International Commission on Human Rights, consisting of experts from several human rights NGOs, and co-ordinated by Africa Watch and the International Federation of Human Rights (Paris), produced more disturbing findings. The Commission found that the Rwandese government had killed about 2,000 Rwandese between October 1990 and January 1993, most of whom were Tutsi or Hutu belonging to opposition parties, and that 'authorities at the highest level, including the President of the Republic, consented to the abuses'.[14]

The International Commission also found that the President and government of Rwanda had 'tolerated and encouraged the activities of armed militia attached to the political parties, in clear violation of Rwandan law'. According to the Commission, by late 1992 these militia had 'taken the lead in violence against Tutsi and members of the political opposition, thus "privatising" violence formerly carried out by the state itself'. Like the reports which had preceded it, the Commission also found the RPF guilty of human rights abuses such as summary executions; the vast majority of its findings, however, incriminated Habyarimana's government.

The Commission's findings prompted the UN to launch its own investigation. Bacre Waly Ndiaye, the Special Rapporteur on Extrajudicial, Summary and Arbitrary Executions for the UN Commission on Human Rights, published his report in August 1993.[15] His findings endorsed those of the Commission. He noted with concern that, following the RPF invasion, government propaganda had created a situation in which 'all Tutsi inside the country were collectively labelled accomplices of the RPF'. This linkage, he concluded, combined with 'the ensuing climate and the directives which followed ... [and] triggered the massacres of civilians'.

The Special Rapporteur even went so far as to note that 'there is a certain elite which, in order to cling to power, is continuing to fuel ethnic hatred'. Again, in addition to the armed forces, the party militias allied to the ruling MRND and the CDR were found to have been guilty of 'incitement to violence against the Tutsi, of massacres of civilian populations and of political assassinations'. He noted reports that 'these militias have been trained by members of the Presidential Guard and by members of the armed forces'.

In addressing the question of the role of ordinary civilians, the Special Rapporteur found that 'such outbreaks were planned and prepared, with targets being identified in speeches by representatives of the authorities, broadcasts on Rwandese radio, and leaflets. It is also noteworthy that at the time of the violence, the persons perpetrating the massacres were under organised leadership. In this connection, local government officials have been found to play a leading role in most cases.' Both the central government and the local authorities were found to have distributed weapons among civilians.

The Special Rapporteur made a number of specific recommendations addressed chiefly to the Rwandese government. These included measures to protect civilians against massacres; support for Rwandese human rights NGOs; reform of the media; reform of the judicial system; new identity cards containing no reference to ethnicity; and the dismantling of all 'violent organisations', including party militias. Not one of these recommendations was acted upon.

Arming the Rwandese regime

At the same time that this evidence of human rights abuses was emerging, several Northern powers were continuing to arm Habyarimana's regime. The USA had been supplying a relatively small quantity of arms since the early 1980s; for the 1993 financial year, US military sales were estimated to be worth $600,000. But South Africa was revealed to have supplied arms worth $5.9 million to the Rwandese government.[16]

France was revealed to have enabled the Rwandese government to buy Egyptian arms worth $6 million. These were supplied during 1992, when evidence of human rights abuses by the Rwandese government was already in the public domain and when France was an observer at the Arusha 'peace talks'. The purchase included 'automatic rifles, mortars, long-range artillery, shoulder-fired rocket launchers, munitions, landmines, and plastic explosives'.[17]

French support for Habyarimana's government dated back to the 1970s, when the two countries signed their first military assistance agreement. But following the RPF invasion in 1990, France had sent its own soldiers and military advisers to Rwanda. The contingent more than doubled from 300 soldiers to over 600, following an RPF offensive in February 1993, and was observed providing artillery support to Rwandese government forces, manning armed checkpoints, and advising the Rwandese army during combat situations.[18]

The Arusha Accords

The Arusha Accords were eventually signed by General Habyarimana and Alexis Kanyarengwe, the leader of the RPF, on 4 August 1993. The combined pressures of the RPF's military gains and international expectations had eventually forced Habyarimana's hand. The Accords committed the Rwandese government to a series of radical reforms: the creation of a transitional government of 22 ministers, of whom five would be from the RPF; the creation of a commission to oversee the return of the refugees, and to ensure their security; the establishment of new armed forces, with the RPF contributing 40 per cent of new troops and 50 per cent of the high command; and the organisation of legislative and parliamentary elections in 1995.

The UN Secretary-General argued that the UN could play an important role in assisting the implementation of the accords. He recommended the establishment of a greatly increased UN presence called the United Nations Assistance Mission for Rwanda (UNAMIR). UNAMIR was approved by the UN Security Council, which passed Resolution 872 on 5 October 1993. This gave the UN force a mandate which included monitoring the ceasefire, general responsibility for security, and the repatriation of refugees; clearing mines and coordinating humanitarian assistance; and investigating non-compliance with the agreement to integrate the armed forces.

UN troops arrive

The first UN forces arrived in Kigali in October 1993. By that time it was already clear that the implementation of the Arusha Accords would be fraught with difficulties. The Accords included a timetable for implementation, according to which the transitional government and national assembly should have been up and running by mid-September. But by November neither the new government nor the new parliament was in place.[19]

The UN force came under the command of General Romeo Dallaire of Canada. By December, UNAMIR consisted of 1,260 personnel, with troops from 19 countries, with by far the largest contingents from Bangladesh (564) and Belgium (424). The UN's most evident achievement during December was to accompany 600 RPF troops to Kigali; their presence, designed to ensure the security of RPF officials, had been agreed in the Arusha Accords.

French troops finally left Rwanda in December 1993, against the wishes of the President. From the outset the participation of the Belgians in UNAMIR had been opposed by the MRND and the CDR, who accused them of favouring the RPF. They claimed that an earlier withdrawal of Belgian troops from northern Rwanda in 1990 had been designed to allow the RPF to make military gains.[20]

Extremists hinder progress

The CDR made no attempt to conceal its opposition to power-sharing with the RPF. Radio/TV Libre des Mille Collines (RTLM), run by the CDR and part-owned by Habyarimana's family, went on air in autumn 1993, declaring that the RPF had returned to restore Tutsi hegemony, branding all Tutsi as RPF supporters, denouncing the Arusha Accords, and exhorting listeners to kill Tutsi civilians. The President did not stop the broadcasts.

The hands of the extremists were strengthened by the October 1993 coup in Burundi. Ever since Independence, Hutu in Rwanda had pointed to the fate of Hutu in Burundi in their attempts to justify excluding Tutsi from power and resisting the return of Tutsi refugees; while conversely in Burundi, Tutsi have used the repression of their fellows in Rwanda to justify continued minority rule and the suppression of Hutu aspirations. Now the Hutu supremacists in Rwanda claimed that the coup in Burundi proved that Tutsi were unwilling to share power, and they characterised the RPF as the vanguard of renewed Tutsi domination.

General Habyarimana benefited from divisions within the opposition, some of which he had fostered, but all of which he would skilfully exploit, playing off one personality against another, and factions against their own parties. First the MDR split between supporters of rival would-be Prime Ministers. Then the Liberal Party was riven by internal divisions over nominations to the transitional government and national assembly. Justin Mugenzi, one of its most prominent leaders, was accused by many in his party of being a covert supporter of the President. He was part of what became known as the 'power factions', pro-Habyarimana groups in each of the divided opposition parties.[21]

With Habyarimana insisting on his nomination lists for the future government and the opposition parties squabbling among themselves, the implementation of the Arusha Accords was further delayed. By February 1994 only one of the main institutions agreed at Arusha — the presidency — yet existed. Neither the new national assembly nor the transitional government was functioning. Habyarimana's 'divide and rule' strategy was successfully undermining the move to power-sharing.

The purges begin

Amid the growing confusion, attacks on human rights activists and opposition politicians increased. In November 1993 Aphonse-Marie Nkubito, the attorney general and president of CLADHO (Collectif des Ligues et Associations de Defense des Droits de l'Homme), narrowly escaped death in a grenade attack.[22] In February 1994 Felicien Gatabazi, a member of the Social Democratic Party, was assassinated, as was Martin Bucyana, the president of the CDR. Mr Gatabazi had publicly claimed that the militias were being trained in two camps, Gabiro (Byumba) and Bigogwe (Ruhengeri), and were being armed by the cabinet secretary of Augustin Bizimana (the Defence Minister).[23]

At the same time it was widely known that the militias possessed death lists. The possible existence of such lists had been alluded to by one human rights organisation as early as February 1992, but by early 1994 the lists were so readily available that individuals could pay the militias to have their names removed.[24] Thus there were numerous unmistakable signs, for anyone who cared to observe them, that violence on a terrifying scale was imminent.

The UN reviews its role

The UN Security Council was fully aware of what was taking place. Not only did they have access to the information contained in the reports by human rights NGOs, but the presence of UNAMIR ensured that the Security Council was fully briefed on developments through regular reports by the Secretary-General. As early as December 1993, Dr Boutros-Ghali had referred to attacks upon civilians in the demilitarised zone in northern Rwanda, and stated that 'a well-armed and reportedly ruthless group was operating in the area, with a view to disrupting or even derailing the peace process'.[25]

By March 1994 UNAMIR's strength had risen to 2,539 personnel. There were now 24 participant countries, although the vast majority of the increased force were Ghanaians (843) and additional soldiers from Bangladesh (the new total was 942). But Dr Boutros-Ghali was fully aware that, despite UNAMIR's increased size, violence was on the increase. His report of 30 March 1994 noted that since December, 'the security situation in Rwanda, and, especially in Kigali, has seriously deteriorated. While most incidents can be attributed to armed banditry, which has been growing as a result of the ready availability of weapons, ethnic and politically motivated crimes, including assassinations and murders, have also increased.'

UNAMIR's original mandate was due to last for six months from October 1993, and was therefore already up for review in April. However, despite Dr Boutros-Ghali's recommendation that its mandate be extended for another six months, UN Security Council member states had from the outset tried to scale down their commitment. Even Resolution 872 had invited the Secretary-General 'to consider ways of reducing the total maximum strength of UNAMIR' and requested him to 'seek economies and ... report regularly on what is achieved in this regard'.

PART THREE: THE RESPONSE TO GENOCIDE

The killings escalate

On 6 April 1994 an aircraft bringing President Habyarimana and President Ntariyamira of Burundi back from talks in Arusha crashed as it came in to land at Kigali airport. Everyone on board was killed. When UNAMIR troops went to investigate, they were denied access to the crash site by Rwandese government forces. The Rwandese government immediately accused Belgian UN troops of having shot the plane down, but in the light of events during previous months, and events after the crash, it appears highly likely that the plane was shot down by forces allied to the MRND and CDR, who were intent on sabotaging the Arusha Accords.

Within the hour following the crash, and prior to its official announcement over the radio, *Interahamwe* militiamen had begun to set up road-blocks in Kigali. During 6 and 7 April, the young men checked the identity cards of passers-by, searching for Tutsi, members of opposition parties, and human rights activists. Anyone belonging to these groups was set upon with machetes and iron bars. Their bleeding bodies lined the road-sides of the city.

By 8 April hundreds of Tutsi civilians and several of Rwanda's most important opposition politicians had been killed. Among the politicians to have lost their lives were Agathe Uwilingyamana, the Prime Minister (MDR); Joseph Kavaruganda, the President of the Constitutional Court; Edouard Ntatsindwa, the Minister of Labour (LP); Frederic Nzamurambaho, the Minister of Agriculture (PSD); and the chairman and vice-chairman of the Liberal Party.[26] Many of the murdered politicians and human rights activists were Hutu.

Anne Mackintosh, then Oxfam's Regional Representative based in Kigali, was staying with colleagues at a Catholic mission in

Gisenyi on 8 April. At about mid-day government soldiers came to the mission and threatened to kill three Rwandese people unless they were given some money. They were given money and then left, but later that afternoon a group of about 100 young men, some of them wearing the party caps of the CDR, swept through the out-buildings. This is Anne Mackintosh's testimony:[27]

They sought out and killed seven members of the Tutsi nurse's family who had been hiding, unknown to us, somewhere in the mission buildings. Those killed included a three-year-old boy, his skull split open with a machete blow, and a pregnant woman whose belly was slit open and the unborn baby exposed. I did not examine these bodies, but two Polish missionaries, who were among those staying at the mission, did. However, we all witnessed the elderly mission cook being beaten to death in the courtyard outside the kitchen.

One of the missionaries, Father Richard, tried to reason with members of the crowd. Eventually, I went out to join him. We talked with a couple of young men who spoke French, and appeared to be the group's leaders, although they admitted they couldn't exercise much control. They explained their 'mission': Tutsi had murdered the President and were trying to take over the country by force, so Tutsi had to die.

After about an hour and a half, the mob left, looting mattresses, beer-crates, and other items as they went. Father Richard and another of the missionaries who was a trained nurse went to see whether any of those who had been attacked were still alive and could be helped. Three of the wounded were still moving, but their injuries were so appalling — their skulls had been split open by machete blows, and the brain tissue exposed — that there was no point in trying to save them. However, a girl of about 14 who had been left for dead was found to be alive, though barely conscious. I helped the nurse lay her down on cushions and dress her wounds.

Later that evening more militiamen arrived, and searched all the rooms. Having failed to find anyone else, they stole some more possessions and left. The following day Belgian soldiers arrived and rescued all the guests at the mission; these people would later leave Rwanda altogether. Anne Mackintosh's testimony illustrates the speed at which the killings began; the role of militiamen and soldiers; the way in which government propaganda was adduced to account for the killings; and the plundering made possible by the threat and use of violence.

The RPF advance — and the government flees Kigali

On 9 April 1994 a new administration was announced by the remnants of the Rwandese government. It was dominated by members of the MRND, CDR, and the 'power factions' of the MRD and Liberal Party. Key members included Theodore Sindikubgabo as President, Augustin Bizimana as Defence Minister, and Jean Kambanda as Prime Minister. The 'interim government' also included Joseph Mugenzi and Agnes Ntamabyaliro, from the Liberal Party.[28]

The outbreak of violence in Kigali prompted RPF soldiers in the city to begin fighting forces allied to the 'interim government'. The bulk of the RPF's armed forces, however, were in the demilitarised zone in northern Rwanda. The fighting in Kigali prompted these RPF troops to begin their advance south towards the city. The first RPF soldiers from the north arrived in Kigali on 13 April, the day on which the 'interim government' fled west to Gitarama.

The UN response

Ten Belgian peacekeepers had been killed in an attempt to protect the Prime Minister. With all Belgian UNAMIR soldiers now blamed for the assassination of General Habyarimana, and all facing death threats, Belgium announced the withdrawal of its entire UNAMIR contingent. Henceforth, UNAMIR confined itself to rescuing foreign nationals, as did the French paratroopers who arrived on 10 April.

Television pictures and newspaper reports of UN forces rescuing foreigners but abandoning Rwandese provoked outrage abroad. Among the fiercest critics of UNAMIR's mandate were aid agencies like Oxfam (UK and Ireland), whose expatriate staff were leaving, but whose Rwandese staff were being refused help. The killings in Kigali and the withdrawal of the Belgian contingent from UNAMIR led the UN to review UNAMIR's role. In his 20 April report to the Security Council, Dr Boutros-Ghali argued that UNAMIR's mandate was no longer relevant, that there was 'no prospect' of a ceasefire, and that the Security Council must choose between three options: an 'immediate and massive' reinforcement of UNAMIR, with a new mandate to impose a ceasefire, restore law and order, and provide security for humanitarian aid deliveries; cutting UNAMIR to 270 troops, with a limited mandate to attempt to secure a ceasefire agreement and to assist in humanitarian relief operations 'to the extent feasible'; and sanctioning UNAMIR's complete withdrawal.

As the Security Council reviewed UNAMIR's role, Oxfam (UK/I) argued that the UN had a moral imperative to respond to the crisis. Oxfam drew a distinction between the fighting between the RPF and the 'interim government', and the massacres being carried out by lightly armed militias against unarmed civilians. Even if the UN could not bring the fighting to an end, Oxfam argued, it could protect thousands of people at risk, by giving UN troops a mandate to protect civilians under threat and providing security for the delivery of humanitarian relief. Many other aid agencies backed the demand for a strengthened UNAMIR, as did the Ugandan government.

But on 21 April the Security Council cut the UN force from 1,700 to 270 personnel. The United States took the lead in advocating this decision. Under Resolution 912, UNAMIR was given a new mandate to 'act as an intermediary between the parties in an attempt to secure a ceasefire'; 'assist in the resumption of humanitarian relief operations to the extent feasible'; and 'monitor and report on developments in Rwanda, including the safety and security of the civilians who sought refuge with UNAMIR'. In practice this decision was never fully implemented, with the result that 444 UN troops stayed on in Kigali.[29]

The decision was immediately condemned by aid agencies and governments. David Bryer, director of Oxfam (UK and Ireland), described it as a 'short-sighted, callous decision', while the British development agency Christian Aid argued that the decision meant that 'fighting will spread unchecked and thousands more will be murdered'.[30] Salim Ahmed Salim, the OAU's Secretary-General, deplored the decision 'to abandon the people of Rwanda ... in spite of the appeals from Africa' and stated that many Africans would interpret it as a 'lack of sufficient concern for African tragic situations'.[31]

The reduction of UNAMIR at first appeared to put in jeopardy the lives of the 15,000 Rwandese in Kigali who had sought refuge with the UN, although the rump UN force which stayed behind did succeed in protecting these people. But the UN's reduction sent a signal to those perpetrating the massacres that, despite its tough talk, the UN was not willing to offer any protection to Rwandese outside Kigali whose lives were in imminent danger. Under these circumstances, the militias were able to carry out their campaign of genocide unopposed (with the exception of areas gradually captured by the RPF).

The massacres

As the UN deliberated over how to respond to the crisis, the extremists' campaign to exterminate their political opponents began to spread throughout the country. After 12 April 1994, by which time the massacres in Kigali had claimed an estimated 10,000 lives, journalists and aid agencies began to report massacres to the east. By 19 April the massacres had spread to the south and west, following the removal of the moderate Hutu prefect in Butare and his replacement by an extremist.

The pattern of events over the following two months was already clear by the end of April. In those areas controlled by the 'interim government', genocide was proceeding with ruthless efficiency. At the same time, a conventional war was being fought between the RPF and soldiers loyal to the 'nterim government'. The RPF advanced quickly, meeting little opposition from 'interim government' forces, who were ill-disciplined, poorly motivated, and unused to fighting a determined enemy.

But the RPF's advance simply could not match the pace at which the militiamen and soldiers were massacring civilians. Across Rwanda, the story was the same. Defenceless men, women, and children were being cut across the neck with machetes, and beaten to death with hoes and iron bars. There are several accounts of victims pleading to be shot, rather than face the terror and agony of being cut to death. Those in danger did their best to flee, but the killers respected no sanctuary; militiamen sought out victims in churches and hospital wards.

Such slaughter took place in home after home, village after village, and region after region. Sometimes the entire Tutsi population of an area fled in terror to a church, in the vain hope that there was safety in numbers. But the militias were actively encouraging Tutsi to gather together, because it made their task easier. As in Rukara,[32] they would surround the church and start by throwing grenades in through the windows. With indiscriminate gunfire, they could kill hundreds of people in a matter of minutes. The militiamen would then move in to finish off their victims with machetes and clubs, returning on subsequent days to ensure that no one had escaped alive.

Most of the killers were known to their victims. They came from the same villages, had attended the same schools, and farmed the same hillsides. The frenzy of killing is inexplicable within any conventional frame of reference. But these young men were convinced that in no other way could they ensure the survival of Hutu; they believed that unless all Tutsi were physically eliminated, they would return to reclaim their powers and privileges. They had been told this not only by RTLM (Radio/Television Libre des Mille Collines), but also by some Hutu intellectuals. They were also told that if they did not cooperate, they were collaborators, and could expect to die. Many of those courageous enough to act according to their consciences paid with their lives.

Many of the massacres were organised. This is the testimony of Claude Sonier, who fled from Butare with his Tutsi wife and family. He describes what happened in Butare at the end of April:

Everything was quiet ... Then a new prefect was appointed, a Hutu from the north. Soon afterwards planes landed with members of the Presidential Guard. The killings began early the next morning. The soldiers and militias started with the men, then went on to massacre children ... Mostly they picked on Tutsi, but Hutu were also targeted. The soldiers got the Interahamwe to dig pits, which they lined with flaming tyres. Men, women, and children were thrown in alive. My mother-in-law, a woman in her sixties, died in this way.[33]

The names of the countless towns and villages where such killings took place will probably be forgotten by the outside world: places such as Butare, Kibuye, Cyangugu, Gisenyi, Kabgayi (Gitarama Prefecture); Kibungo, Kibeho (Gikongoro Prefecture); Cyahinda (Butare Prefecture); and Gikongoro. But they will not be forgotten by Rwandese, who will have to return to their former homes to rebuild their lives, surrounded by the evidence of carnage. Their memories will outlast even the mass graves.

Refugee crises in Tanzania and Burundi

As the RPF advanced south and east through Rwanda in April and May 1994, tens of thousands of people fled before them. The vast majority of these people were ordinary Hutu, long-time targets of government propaganda, which had succeeded in instilling the belief that the rebels were intent on killing them. To these people, the RPF's assurances to the contrary meant nothing. They left with whatever food and possessions they could carry, and sometimes with their cattle. In their midst were militiamen responsible for the massacres.

Displaced people fled from eastern Rwanda into Tanzania. On 29 April over 200,000 people crossed the Rusumo Falls bridge over the Kagera river into Ngara District in Tanzania — the fastest flow of refugees that aid agencies had ever witnessed. Over the coming weeks the number of refugees in Tanzania would swell to 470,000. The main refugee camp in this area, at Benaco, would become home to 250,000 people, making it the largest refugee camp in the world. The UNHCR and several other aid agencies worked together to provide food, equipment, and health care. Oxfam (UK/I), which has particular expertise in the provision of safe water, is the lead agency supplying water to these refugees.

Thousands of people were also leaving eastern Rwanda farther north, crossing into the Karagwe district of Tanzania, and in the south, into Burundi. In Burundi, they arrived in camps where the UNHCR and other aid agencies, including Oxfam, were working. In subsequent weeks the number of refugees would continue to escalate. But, while those who had become refugees received assistance, over one million displaced people within Rwanda faced a desperate struggle for survival; while the true figure may never be known, it seems likely that thousands died from exhaustion, starvation, and disease.

The agency with legal responsibility for the refugees' welfare was the UNHCR, which co-ordinated the relief work in the camps. The UN's Department of Humanitarian Affairs set up an emer-gency office in Nairobi (UN Rwanda Emergency Office — UNREO) to pool information on the work of all the UN agencies and NGOs, and sent an assessment mission to Kigali. However, the insecurity within Rwanda prevented most of them from working there. Only the International Committee for the Red Cross (ICRC), Médecins Sans Frontières, and a number of mission NGOs actually carried on working in Rwanda. They struggled valiantly under desperate conditions, while gangs periodically roamed hospital wards at will, killing patients and Rwandese staff alike.

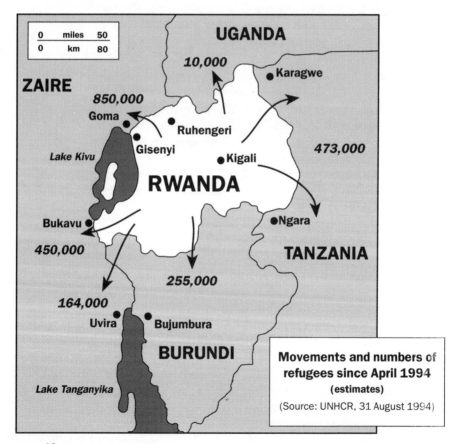

Movements and numbers of refugees since April 1994
(estimates)
(Source: UNHCR, 31 August 1994)

The case for a new UN force

The rump UN force in Kigali, under the command of General Dallaire, succeeded in protecting 15,000 civilians, by delivering relief supplies and negotiating with their attackers when they were under threat. These people were scattered at a number of locations in Kigali, in hospitals, the Hotel des Mille Collines, and the Amahoro stadium. UNAMIR also evacuated groups in particular danger, including orphans.[34]

The UN also tried to negotiate with the RPF and the 'interim government' to secure a ceasefire. The RPF refused to have anything to do with the 'interim government', whom it dismissed as 'a clique of killers'. The RPF declared that it would not talk about a ceasefire until the 'interim government' had called a halt to the massacres; the 'interim government', for its part, asserted that the main problem was the rebel advance. No progress towards a ceasefire was achieved.

By the end of April 1994 aid agencies feared that 200,000 people had been killed in Rwanda; well over one million were known to be internally displaced, and hundreds of thousands had become refugees in neighbouring countries. As the scale of the crisis became ever more apparent, the UN came under increasing pressure to send a new peacekeeping force to protect civilians under threat. As the Secretary-General began to review Resolution 912, governments, aid agencies, and journalists began to exert pressure for a speedy UN response.

Among those calling for a new UN force were the OAU and African countries such as Tanzania. Ali Hassan Mwinyi, President of Tanzania, argued that 'Where the very survival of humanity is at stake, where the outbreak and level of violence reaches enormous proportions to threaten the very fabric of human civilisation and where ethnic conflicts might threaten international peace, the United Nations must be able to act

41

promptly and decisively.' He urged the UN to take 'firm action' to stop the 'senseless killings'.[35]

Oxfam (UK/I) asserted the case for vigorous UN action. Through a series of vigils and advertisements, Oxfam raised public awareness of genocide in Rwanda, and lobbied decision-makers with specific proposals for a new UN force, designed to save civilian lives and enable aid agencies to provide humanitarian aid. In pursuance of Oxfam's advocacy, David Bryer and Ed Cairns, policy adviser, met Dr Boutros-Ghali on 5 May to put the agency's case directly.

On 13 May Dr Boutros-Ghali recommended a new UN force to the Security Council, which would consist of 5,500 troops (UNAMIR II), with a mandate to protect civilians under threat and help to provide humanitarian aid to the displaced. He stressed that the force should be sent to the interior of Rwanda, as well as to its borders, because there were five times as many displaced people in the interior itself. He also stressed that the longer the troops' deployment was delayed, 'the greater the prospect of the mission not achieving its purpose in operational terms'.[36]

Dr Boutros-Ghali's plan envisaged UN troops first taking control of Kigali airport and then fanning out across Rwanda to establish protected sites for the displaced. His timetable would have seen the Ghanaian battalion brought up to its full strength of 800 men within a week of the Security Council's authorisation; and the rest of the 5,500 troops establishing their presence within 31 days. If the Security Council swiftly approved the plan, and countries quickly supplied troops and the means to put them in place, a revitalised UNAMIR could be saving lives in Rwanda by the beginning of June, and throughout the country by the middle of June.

The response of the Security Council

From the outset, the Permanent Five Members of the Security Council ruled out sending any of their own troops. The question then was whether other countries would offer troops, and the nature of the mandate that the Security Council would give them.

Just as it had taken the lead in advocating UNAMIR's reduction, the USA took the lead in pressing for a plan that would confine UNAMIR to the borders of Rwanda. The United States also sought to play down the scale of the crisis, by instructing its officials to use the phrase 'acts of genocide', rather than acknowledge that a deliberate policy of genocide was being implemented.[37] The alleged reason for this word-play was that the US government feared that acknowledging this would oblige it to undertake more vigorous action under the UN's Convention on Genocide.

Under the terms of Article II of the Convention on the Prevention and Punishment of Genocide (1948), genocide is defined as:

any of the following acts committed with intent to destroy, in whole or in part, a national, ethnical, racial or religious group, as such: killing members of the group; causing serious bodily or mental harm to members of the group; deliberately inflicting on the group conditions of life calculated to bring about its physical destruction in whole or in part; imposing measures intended to prevent births within the group; and forcibly transferring children of the group to another group.

That the killings in Rwanda met this definition was later confirmed by R. Degni-Segui, the Special Rapporteur on Human Rights, in a report to the UN. He had been appointed by a Special Session of the UN Commission on Human Rights which had met in May. The Genocide Convention commits parties to the Convention to 'prevent and punish' genocide, whether committed in time of peace or war. All five permanent members of the Security Council have ratified the Genocide Convention.

The mandate of UNAMIR II

Dr Boutros-Ghali's efforts to get Security Council backing for a new initiative eventually met with success. On 16 May the Security Council passed Resolution 918, adopting the plan which the Secretary-General had advocated in his report. UNAMIR II, when it arrived, would 'attempt to assure the security of as many assemblies as possible of civilians who are under threat' and would 'provide security, as required, to humanitarian relief operations'. According to Dr Boutros-Ghali's original timetable, it would still be possible to see all 5,500 troops carrying out their mandate by the middle of June. The resolution also imposed an arms embargo on Rwanda, under Chapter 7 of the UN Charter.

At about the same time, several African countries indicated their willingness to provide troops. They were Ethiopia, Ghana, Senegal, Malawi, Mali, Zambia, and Zimbabwe. Tanzania and Zaire also offered troops, but the OAU's rules prevent member states from sending troops to neighbouring countries. However, the troops lacked the equipment and logistical support to mount a speedy operation.

Having refused to send their own troops, Security Council members now failed even to deliver the means by which African troops could be sent. Their response, the US offer to loan 50 armoured vehicles, and the UK offer to supply 50 trucks, was totally inadequate, coming as it did from governments with two of the best-equipped military forces in the world. But some African governments also failed Rwanda, by making 'exorbitant demands for their battalions', instead of making reasonable requests.[38]

These failures delayed the deployment of UN forces still further. By the end of May, with not a single extra UN soldier in Rwanda, Dr Boutros-Ghali boldly criticised UN member states. He deplored the fact that the international community 'appears paralysed in reacting', almost two months after the start of the killings, 'even to the revised mandate' given by the Security Council:

We must all recognise that ... we have failed in our response to the agony of Rwanda, and thus have acquiesced in the continued loss of human lives. Our readiness and our capacity for action has been demonstrated to be inadequate at best, and deplorable at worst, owing to the absence of collective political will.[39]

The French intervention

By mid-June 1994 aid agencies estimated that genocide had cost over 500,000 lives; about two million people were internally displaced, and over half a million had fled to neighbouring countries. This was a catastrophe unprecedented in Africa, and the massacres continued, unabated and unchecked. By this time the entire UNAMIR II force should have been in place, but still not a single extra peacekeeper had arrived.

In mid-June, France suddenly announced its intention to send 2,500 troops to Rwanda — a strictly humanitarian mission, according to the French government. The soldiers' objective would be to save civilian lives, by establishing a 'safe zone' in the south-west. Many countries, aid agencies (including Oxfam), and journalists expressed concern, arguing that, as France had armed the former government and helped to train its soldiers, it was ill-placed to launch a humanitarian mission. If France genuinely wanted to help, they argued, it should provide the African soldiers already offered to UNAMIR with the means to do so.

The RPF was implacably opposed to the French initiative, seeing France as partly responsible for the massacres, and intent on propping up the remnants of the old regime, to boost its position at future negotiations. Suspicion was fostered not only by French actions in the past, but by reports that in May the French had turned a blind eye to arms bound for 'interim government' forces arriving in Goma, Zaire,[40] and were using deniable agents to supply arms to the 'interim government' as late as June.[41]

By mid-June, the RPF had secured the whole of eastern Rwanda. In most areas (but notably not Kigali), the Rwandese army and allied militias had simply fled. The rebels now planned to consolidate their gains in the south and west, precisely the area into which the French proposed to send troops. If French soldiers resisted its advance, the RPF threatened that it would fight them.

Operation Turquoise

France, however, was determined that 'Operation Turquoise' would go ahead. By drawing on its forces in the Central African Republic, France had mobilised over 1,000 soldiers within days; they were ready and waiting on the border with Rwanda, in bases at Bukavu and Goma in Zaire. France declared, however, that it wanted the Security Council's endorsement, which it duly received on 22 June. Ten out of the fifteen Security Council Members had backed the plan; none of the Permanent Five had used its veto, but China had abstained, as had four non-permanent members: Brazil, New Zealand, Nigeria, and Pakistan.

From their bases in Zaire, the French sent missions into western Rwanda, starting with Cyangugu in the south and Kibuye farther north. Over the coming days the French troops rescued thousands of people: nuns who had hidden in terror, orphans who had wandered in aimless desperation, and men who had hidden for weeks in the forests. But the soldiers swiftly discovered that they had come too late to save most of the vulnerable: the majority of the region's Tutsi had already been killed.[42]

The area around Gishyita (Kibuye Prefecture), for example, had been home to 10,000 Tutsi; now, estimated Eric Nzabihimana, a local schoolteacher, there were fewer than 1,000.[43] Nothing had prepared even the soldiers for the scenes of horror that awaited them. But they would also witness remarkable acts of courage, as in Gikongoro, where a Hutu family had hidden 21 Tutsi in their home since the start of the fighting.

The 'safe area' also reassured the 1,500,000 displaced people living there that it was safe to stay, thus preventing a mass exodus into Zaire. The anticipated conflict between the rebels and the French soldiers never materialised. In practice, the rebels largely ignored the safe area, and concentrated on capturing the few remaining areas of Rwanda under 'interim government' control. In early July they finally took Kigali, and then Butare, the second-largest city, in the south. Now the only area denied them was the north-west; this would be the focus of their final push for victory.

The refugee crisis in Zaire

As the RPF advanced across the north-west, reports began to emerge of hundreds of thousands of Hutu fleeing westward. On 9 July, Maurice Herson, an Oxfam Emergencies Officer on an assessment mission in western Rwanda, reported that 'the entire population is being squeezed west ... We have no idea how many people stay behind — apart from those incapable of moving, the very old, the handicapped, any young abandoned or lost children — nor what happens to them if they do stay. The important point is that they believe they will be massacred. Thus they run.'[44]

Despite numerous RPF assurances that they had nothing to fear from a rebel victory, Hutu were convinced that the rebels would exact reprisals. These fears were deliberately exploited by remnants of the 'interim government' and their soldiers and militias, living among the displaced. They gave chilling accounts of RPF massacres, for which little evidence existed, and exhorted their terrified listeners to flee before they were slaughtered. The extremist radio station, RTLM, reinforced this message with broadcasts urging people to show solidarity with the 'interim government' by fleeing with it.

On 9 July, some newspapers began to cover the story.[45] Aid agencies working in Rwanda had been aware for a number of weeks that a rebel push in the north-west would result in massive displacement, but no one could predict with confidence the direction in which people would go. UNHCR, with its mandate to address the relief needs of refugees, was not responsible for meeting the needs of the displaced; as long as people stayed inside Rwanda, other agencies were expected to cater for them. UNREO, the UN office nominally co-ordinating the relief effort, was not an operational agency; rather, its function was to pool information so that the aid agencies were aware of what was going on and could act accordingly.

A calamity without precedent

When the RPF took Ruhengeri, and the 'interim government' forces decamped to Gisenyi, NGOs began to report a human tide, greater even than that which had descended upon Tanzania. Some 10,000 people were crossing the border into Goma every hour, the fastest exodus ever witnessed by aid agencies. Johanna Grombach, head of the ICRC in Goma, described the situation on 14 July as 'a humanitarian catastrophe'. 'The needs are just too much,' she said. 'We cannot feed all these people. The medical needs are also enormous.'[46]

One million Rwandese descended on Zaire in the space of a few days. They had arrived after days of walking across mountainous terrain, exhausted and dehydrated, and desperate to eat, drink, and rest. Many simply lay down and died. In subsequent days, cholera would claim many lives; but the biggest killers appear to have been dysentery and diarrhoea, combined with exhaustion, dehydration, and malnutrition. Soon, two thousand people were dying every day:[47] one person every minute, of every hour. The death rates were without precedent in aid agencies' experience, far higher than any that had been faced elsewhere.

Aid agencies unprepared

The Goma crisis found aid agencies unprepared. Those with teams already in place were the International Committee of the Red Cross, MSF–Holland, Oxfam (UK and Ireland), Caritas, and the UNHCR; but no agency had predicted the sheer scale of the crisis, nor planned and prepared accordingly. The lack of preparedness meant that immediate needs went unmet; pre-positioned food stocks were enough for only a small fraction of the refugee population, and there was no equipment in place to provide safe water.[48]

But the state of unreadiness also led to decisions being taken that exacerbated the already desperate situation. The choice of sites for refugees was one such example. Because Goma town was so over-crowded, refugees had to be sent elsewhere. Tragically, people were directed northwards towards Katale, where there was no surface water on their route, rather than west, which would have given them access to water (from Lake Kivu) on their journey. As one journalist would put it, 'It was a decision that was effectively to pass a death sentence on many people.'[49]

There was further confusion over whether refugees should be encouraged to return to Rwanda, or whether the situation in Zaire should be stabilised first. Different agencies disagreed with each other, and the UN's policy appeared to change several times. What was clear to all the agencies was that their combined capacity was too small for their enormous task; on 18 July Oxfam argued that only a massive and immediate airlift could hope to improve the situation.

The problem of co-ordination

UNHCR, having taken over responsibility for those in need once they had crossed into Zaire, allocated different tasks to different agencies. By 20 July, many NGOs had established a presence, but most of the work was carried out by ICRC (food supplies), MSF (health care), Oxfam (water supplies) and CARE (non-food items). Later, the World Food Programme took the lead in trucking and flying food to Goma. As the news media began to cover the situation in Goma, more and more governments offered funds and practical help, including the USA, the UK, France, Germany, the Netherlands, and New Zealand.

While these offers were widely welcomed, the operational effectiveness of these initiatives was compromised by the unwillingness of some governments to consult and co-ordinate with the aid agencies already in place. Nicholas Stockton, Oxfam's Emergencies Co-ordination Manager, gave one example of two different approaches:

The build-up of the international relief response is moving with extreme rapidity, although unco-ordinated bilateral decision-making in many national capitals and the headquarters of international aid organisations is causing enormous confusion on the ground. ... From our discussions here with GTZ [German technical aid department], it appears that their interpretation of 'tasking' implies that they take full responsibility for the water and sanitation sector, a role which will include funding existing work of NGOs, as well as adding new operational components of their own. In contrast, the officer in charge of the US water project in Goma said, 'I take my orders from Mannheim' [the US military base in Germany], and he appears to have no interest in or understanding of the word 'co-ordination'. This is also the style of the French and Israeli military teams here, and is presumably a function of military management.[50]

Not only was co-ordination lacking, but the water-purification equipment supplied by the US military was inappropriate to the task. The equipment they flew in was designed to provide high-quality water for small numbers of people; whereas what was actually needed was safe water for hundreds of thousands of people. However, the USA did provide two fire engines which enabled large quantities of water to be pumped out of Lake Kivu. Unfortunately, no one had ensured that there were sufficient tankers to deliver it.[51]

Despite the will to help, far too little was actually achieved in the vital early weeks of the crisis, and death rates continued at unprecedented levels. With about 2,000 people dying every day, much time was consumed simply in burying the dead. By the end of July, 40 truckloads of bodies were being transported out of the camps every day. Bodies lay unregarded in fields, and were stacked three to four deep by the road-sides. French soldiers collected bodies in Goma itself, but in Kibumba camp to the north, young Zairean Boy Scouts undertook this horrific task.

Oxfam soon took responsibility for providing safe water, and by the first week of August had established a water supply for hundreds of thousands of refugees. As the aid agencies continued their work in the camps, governments had come forward with offers of troops for a UN force. The United Kingdom, which had spent £45 million on aid for Rwanda since April, had announced an increase of £10 million, and offered 600 troops to improve logistical support within the country. Other countries to offer troops were Canada, Australia, Ethiopia, and Zimbabwe. The USA had announced that 200 troops would be sent to Kigali to open up the airport and assist in the distribution of relief supplies within Rwanda, operating outside the UN force.

The RPF, having established control throughout Rwanda (with the exception of the French zone) when it took Gisenyi on 18 July, had announced the formation of a transitional government. The new Rwandese government signalled its intention to work with Hutu by appointing Faustin Twagiramungu as Prime Minister, and Pasteur Bizimungu as President. The new government did not contain Hutu from northern Rwanda, the former President's power base.

Events during August 1994

Despite numerous assurances from the new government that Hutu would be welcomed back to Rwanda, in early August only a few thousand refugees were returning each day, out of a total population of one million. Some agencies were tempted to encourage the refugees to return. But, apart from the fact that many were too weak to make the journey, most were far too frightened to consider an early return, fearing reprisals from RPF soldiers.

There were also security considerations, which were in danger of being ignored, as Oxfam's Nicholas Stockton pointed out from Goma: 'The political realities here lead us to believe quite strongly that a badly organised and poorly screened repatration ... almost certainly will lead to a rapid increase in insecurity in Rwanda, as guerrillas are infiltrated into the country who will enjoy popular support of people in the Gisenyi and Ruhengeri area.'[52]

During early August, death rates in the camps around Goma began to decline; by 10 August they were down to 500 a day, and by the end of August the toll was 300 a day. The Goma crisis, however, had cost at least 46,000 lives.[53] Meanwhile, it was becoming clear that militiamen in the camps were spreading propaganda to terrify the refugees into staying. This soon became a major obstacle to an early return.

French troops had begun a phased withdrawal from south-western Rwanda during August, and by 22 August had pulled out completely. Aid agencies feared a sudden exodus from the south-west in Zaire, but it was not forthcoming. None the less, about 450,000 Rwandese had left Rwanda for the Bukavu area of Zaire by the end of August.

By early September, UNAMIR II was approaching the size which Dr Boutros-Ghali had envisaged for it in May, with 4,167 personnel in Rwanda. The largest contingents came from Ghana (819), Ethiopia (800), the United Kingdom (606), Canada (394), Australia (312), and Senegal (241); but troops had also been sent by Malawi, Nigeria, Chad, Zambia, Tunisia, Niger, Congo, and Guinea Bissau.

At the same time, the first reports emerged of revenge killings against refugees returning from neighbouring countries.[54] Although these were condemned by the new government, it was not easy for it to stop people taking the law into their own hands.

Prospects for the future

Even before the campaign of genocide and the refugee crises of 1994, Rwanda was one of the world's poorest countries. Today, Rwanda barely exists as a nation state. The latest estimates suggest that up to one million Rwandese were killed in the genocide; and, while two million of its citizens languish in refugee camps in neighbouring countries, over one million displaced people struggle to survive in Rwanda itself. Over half of the former population of 7.2 million are therefore either dead, displaced, or living as refugees.

Physically, much of the country has been destroyed, including homes, schools, businesses, infrastructure, and swathes of forest. It may now take decades before Rwanda returns to the standard of living of the early 1980s. It will now be vital for the Rwandese government to devise its own plan for national rehabilitation and reconstruction **(Recommendation 1a)**. The onus will then be on the international community to fully fund this plan and to provide any practical assistance requested by the Rwandese government **(1b)**. One major issue will be the re-establishment of central and local government. At the same time, the Rwandese people will continue to need urgent relief aid from the international community **(1c)**.

The refugee crises of 1994 have dramatically compounded an already highly complex refugee situation. The history of the region demonstrates the dangers inherent in a large Rwandese refugee population remaining in neighbouring countries. The former government and its soldiers and militias appear to be planning to return to Rwanda by force. Unless the Rwandese government and regional powers can forge a political solution that is acceptable to the majority of refugees, further violence and even war remain all too probable. The principles of regional co-operation, and power-sharing in Rwanda, were set down in the

Arusha Accords. These principles should now form the foundations of a regional political settlement **(2a)**.

There are other dangers resulting from the presence of tens of thousands of refugees in surrounding countries. In areas of land shortage, such as Kivu, resentment against Rwandese refugees could easily ignite violent conflict, as it has done in the recent past. This could have devastating consequences for the stability of the Great Lakes region. But in Tanzania, it is at least possible that a durable solution to the Rwandese refugee issue lies not in the refugees' return, but in their resettlement and naturalisation.

The refugees now in surrounding countries are unlikely to return to Rwanda unless they have a stake in their country's future. The new Rwandese government includes Hutu from southern Rwanda, but none from northern Rwanda, the former President's power base. Yet, because Rwanda's politics has a strong regional dimension (see Part Two), and because many of the refugees came from northern Rwanda, the presence of moderate Hutu from northern Rwanda in the Rwandese government may be crucial if refugees are to be encouraged to return **(2b)**.

At the same time, the refugees need to be persuaded that they will not face reprisals on returning to Rwanda, and that they will be able to reclaim their land and property. If revenge killings are to be prevented, the Rwandese government will need to establish law and order throughout the country. To that end, it is currently struggling to put in place a new legal and judicial system. Practical assistance from the international community will be vital **(2c)**, and the urgent deployment of human rights monitors **(2d)**. At the same time, a full-strength UNAMIR II could also help to assure refugees of their safety **(2e)**.

The new government has announced its intention to prosecute suspected war criminals, and all governments are obliged by the Genocide Convention to assist in this process. There are now two UN Commissions investigating the role of individuals in perpetrating genocide, but they are seriously under-resourced, and will require extra resources if they are to perform their functions effectively **(2f)**. Once these Commissions have reported, the next step will be to establish a judicial process. If refugees are to be persuaded that it is safe to return, it will be vital for the judicial process to be fair and transparent. The Rwandese government has accepted the principle of an international judicial process; this will require international backing if it is to be established **(2g)**.

Rwanda's long-term development, and the work of NGOs such as Oxfam, will depend vitally upon whether peace is secured in the region. Further measures to promote peace would be to encourage the government of Zaire to fulfil its pledge to disarm the army of the former government **(3a)**; to ensure that the arms embargo put in place by Resolution 918 is properly enforced **(3b)**; and to provide development aid to communities in neighbouring countries **(3c)**, whose local environments have been dramatically effected by the massive influx of Rwandese refugees.

The prospects for peace in Rwanda will be greatly affected by developments in Burundi. In the past, the fortunes of Hutu and Tutsi in Rwanda have had a direct impact upon Hutu and Tutsi in Burundi, and *vice versa*. The same is likely to be true in the future. It will thus be vital to prevent violent conflict from escalating in Burundi, and the international community should investigate measures to support this **(4a,b)**. More important, however, will be the political initiatives undertaken by the Burundese government.

In both the short and long terms, the region as a whole will have to address the issues of refugees, migrants, economic co-operation, and the promotion of peace. The OAU, which played a vital role in past efforts to resolve the refugee situation, may have an important role to play now. The region's problems are not unique; similar issues are being faced all over Africa. If these challenges are to be met, vigorous political will on the part of African and Northern governments will be absolutely imperative.

Lessons from the international response

The primary responsibility for genocide in Rwanda and the current refugee crisis lies with those extremists who sought to sabotage the Arusha Accords by attempting to eliminate their political opposition. Having slaughtered up to one million people, mostly Tutsi, they encouraged Hutu, already terrified of the advancing rebel army, to flee abroad. They also bear primary responsibility, therefore, for the deaths of at least 50,000 Rwandese refugees in neighbouring countries.

However, the international community, and in particular the most powerful member states of the United Nations, have, through their complacency and inaction, contributed to the slaughter in Rwanda. They failed to heed the warning signs, when it became clear that extremists were trying to undermine the Arusha Accords. And they failed to put sufficient pressure on the Rwandese government to comply with the recommendations of a UN Special Rapporteur, who warned of the insidious effect of government propaganda against Tutsi, and revealed massacres organised by government officials and carried out by the militias.

The political will was apparently lacking; a message underlined by the fact that, from the very date UNAMIR was established on 5 October 1993, right up until the end of March 1994, when the fragility of the Arusha Accords was abundantly clear, the Security Council asked the Secretary- General to cut the size of the UN force in order to save money. This lack of political will also underlies the international community's failure to mount an effective response to subsequent developments in Rwanda.

Oxfam believes that the Rwandese people have the same basic rights as all other people throughout the world, and that the international community has a moral obligation to protect and promote these fundamental rights. One way of achieving greater consistency in international action to uphold basic rights would be to agree principles and criteria for specific UN responses when civilians are threatened by intra-state and inter-state conflict **(5)**.

But the starting point for any attempt by the international community to uphold basic rights, and to undertake better conflict prevention, is the need to be properly informed of threats to peace and security. If serious consideration is to be given to conflict prevention, the UN needs an Office of Preventive Diplomacy **(6a)**, and the Security Council's agreement to consider appropriate preventive action in response to its reports **(6b)**. Where detailed 'on the ground' information is lacking, UN human rights monitors should be available for immediate deployment **(6c)**.

In the case of Rwanda, however, external powers, including France and the United States, supplied arms to the then government, despite the evidence of gross violations of human rights, and despite being observers to the Arusha 'peace process'. Unless there is greater transparency in arms supplies, there will be no possibility of public debate about which foreign governments should receive military assistance; ensuring that arms supplies are registered with the UN's Register of Conventional Arms is one way in which transparency could be enhanced **(7a)**.

This register could be extended to include small arms, such as automatic weapons, which are currently not covered by the Register, but claim many lives in the developing world. In the long term, an international code of conduct on the transfer, sale, and export of arms could be established. This would reduce arms supplies to governments which violate the basic rights of their citizens **(7b)**.

Some of the arms exported to the former government and the RPF continue to claim lives to this day. They are the anti-personnel mines, which were used by both the former government and the RPF during the civil war which followed the RPF's invasion in 1990. As refugees return from neighbouring countries, they are being maimed and killed by these indiscriminate weapons. Oxfam believes that the only effective way to prevent the use of mines is to ban their production, sale, export, transfer, stockpiling, and use **(7c)**.

The international community's response to events following the assassination of President Habyarimana, points the way to equally important lessons. Belgium swiftly withdrew its entire UNAMIR contingent after ten of its peacekeepers were killed. With the best equipped soldiers gone, the Security Council drastically cut the UN force to less than a quarter of its previous size. UN member states then swiftly evacuated their own citizens, leaving desperate Rwandese to their terrible fate.

The major powers in the Security Council then deliberately delayed the establishment of a new UN peacekeeping force. The United States, the world's only remaining superpower, took the lead in this shameful abdication of responsibility.[55] Its officials refused to acknowledge that genocide was taking place, and lobbied to restrict the new UN force to the border areas of Rwanda, when there was clear evidence that the majority of those under threat were within Rwanda itself.

When the new UN force was eventually agreed (nearly six weeks after the killings had begun), the most powerful UN member states failed to offer troops. But when African countries came forward to contribute their own soldiers, Northern states with the greatest military capacities failed to provide sufficient equipment and logistical support to put these peacekeepers in place. However, some African governments sought to exploit this situation for their own ends, instead of taking their own initiatives.

Two countries which did demonstrate the will to act were Ghana and Ethiopia. Ghana provided the bulk of the peacekeepers who remained in Rwanda, and these two countries provide the largest UN contingents in UNAMIR II. But the exception proves the rule. The result of this failure was that, in July 1994, nearly three months after the killings had begun, UNAMIR II had still not arrived in Rwanda. The genocide thus proceeded unabated and unopposed (with the exception of areas gradually taken by the RPF) and, until the French arrived in late July, no one was present to reassure displaced people that it was safe to stay.

It is unrealistic to suggest that a UN force of 5,500 men could have brought the killings in Rwanda to an immediate halt. The speed and scale of the slaughter was such that even had this force arrived by mid-June (as originally planned by the Secretary-General), hundreds of thousands of Rwandese would have lost their lives. And, once the force was in place, it would have taken time for it to protect civilians effectively.

But the lame excuses of governments, including the most powerful Security Council members, have been given the lie by the successful protection of thousands of civilians by the rump UN force that remained in Kigali, by the ability of French troops to restore security in the south-west, and by the speed with which Security Council members have deployed troops when they chose to act, in response to the refugee crisis in Goma.

France, and now the USA and the UK, have proved that it is possible to send troops within days if there is the political will. They were unwilling to enable African peacekeepers to be deployed in Rwanda at an early stage, but have proved capable of prompt action when it suits them. So the claim that a UN force could not have saved many thousands of lives, and could not have been put in place quickly — the claim, in effect, that what has happened in Rwanda was somehow inevitable — is entirely contradicted by the facts.

The ability of the rump UN force in Kigali to save the lives of thousands of civilians has a wide significance. It suggests that the policy of caution about UN peacekeeping, induced by experience in Somalia, should now be reviewed; it appears that if UN troops are given a mandate to protect civilians, rather than to engage in offensive military actions (as in Somalia), it is possible for them to achieve a great deal, even in very adverse circumstances.

If the UN is to mount a speedy and effective response to similar emergencies in the future, Security Council members will have to demonstrate a renewed commitment to UN peacekeeping. The UN's readiness to mount peacekeeping operations should be improved by member states committing more troops and equipment under the existing stand-by arrangements, and by adapting these arrangements to embrace Chapters 6 and 7 of the UN Charter (at present they encompass only Chapter 6) **(8a)**.

By providing advance peacekeeping training to troops offered under these arrangements, UN member states with the greatest military capacity and expertise could increase the supply of well-trained UN peacekeepers, ready to be deployed **(8b)**. In the short term, UN member states should also improve the financing of UN peacekeeping **(8c,d,e)**.

In the long term, UN member states should establish a rapid deployment force, to undertake peacekeeping operations in emerging crises **(9)**. This force should be large enough to undertake the range of operations that might be required, but could be reinforced or replaced by conventional UN peace-keepers if that proved necessary. The main rationale for such a force is that early and effective UN involvement can prevent conflicts from escalating beyond the point at which peace can be swiftly restored.

It became clear from the tragedy in Goma that the international community is desperately ill-prepared to cope with humanitarian emergencies. Although the Goma crisis was unprecedented in its urgency, the international response exhibited failures on several key issues: planning and preparation in advance of the crisis; the capacity of the aid agencies to address it; the lack of expertise among national military teams about the specific demands of humanitarian emergencies; the lack of consultation and co-ordination by some of the actors involved in the relief effort. The UN should now publicly evaluate the performance of its departments and agencies, in their response to the Goma crisis, to establish what lessons can be learnt **(10a)**.

In the short term, UN Consolidated Appeals should be fully funded and the Department of Humanitarian Affairs given the authority to co-ordinate the actions of the various agencies responding to an emergency **(10b,c)**. In the long term, an effective emergency machinery might involve creating one single UN Department responsible for emergencies, incorporating the existing functions of the DHA and those of the operational UN agencies **(10d)**. This department could be responsible for collecting early-warning information and making needs assessments, and for organising and undertaking the emergency response itself.

The department could thus ensure a wholly co-ordinated and effective response on the part of the UN, and provide a single point of reference for NGOs and governments responding to the same emergency. It would need to be given a senior status within the UN system, hence the suggestion that it be headed by a Deputy Secretary-General. The mandate of this Department should cover the internally displaced as well as refugees, so that the response to human suffering need not wait until the threat of a refugee crisis has become a reality **(10e)**.

Recommendations

Oxfam (UK/I) will continue its work in Rwanda and the Great Lakes region with a major programme of relief work in the years to come. Whether that programme will be able to achieve a transition to development work will depend, above all, on the willingness and ability of the Rwandese government and regional powers to forge a political solution to the challenges that confront them. But the international community can also play an important role in Rwanda's recovery, and enhance the prospects of peace throughout the Great Lakes region.

Oxfam believes that the government of Rwanda, the regional powers, and the international community should actively consider the following recommendations:

1 to foster Rwanda's recovery:

   a. *the government of Rwanda*: by developing a rehabilitation and reconstruction plan that will receive the backing of the international community;

   b. *the international community*: by funding this rehabilitation and reconstruction plan and by providing any practical assistance requested by the Rwandese government;

   c. *the international community*: by funding efforts to provide relief to Rwandese refugees in neighbouring countries, to the displaced inside Rwanda, and to returning refugees;

2 to promote reconciliation between all Rwandese people, and a climate for the return of refugees:

   a. *the government of Rwanda and the regional powers*: by forging a political solution to the challenges that face them, based upon the principles of power-sharing and regional co-operation in the Arusha Accords;

   b. *the government of Rwanda*: by sharing political and military power with moderate Hutu, including Hutu from northern Rwanda;

c. *the international community*: by assisting the Rwandese government in its efforts to establish a new legal and judicial system;

d. *the international community*: by sending UN human rights monitors to every commune in Rwanda, to accompany returning refugees;

e. *the international community*: by ensuring that UNAMIR II reaches its full strength and is fully funded once in place;

f. *the international community*: by strengthening the UN Commissions which are investigating the role of individuals in perpetrating genocide;

g. *the international community*: by establishing an international judicial process to prosecute individuals suspected of crimes against humanity, including genocide, an other gross violations of human rights;

3 to promote peace and development in the region:

a. *the government of Zaire*: by fulfilling its commitment to disarm former Rwandese government soldiers within its borders;

b. *the international community*: by ensuring that the arms embargo established by Resolution 918 is properly enforced;

c. *the international community*: by providing development aid to the communities in Tanzania, Zaire, Burundi, and Uganda that have been affected by the recent influx of Rwandese refugees;

4 to prevent violent conflict from escalating in Burundi:

a. *the international community*: by sending human rights monitors to Burundi, to investigate the current situation and establish recommendations for further action;

b. *the international community:* by sending international monitors to Burundi to join the OAU's observation mission to monitor the activities of the security forces;

The international response to the crises in Rwanda suggests that a major reform of the UN's peacekeeping and emergency capacities is now needed, if effective action is to be taken in response to similar crises in the future. This is above all a question of the political will among UN member states.

Oxfam believes that the international community should actively consider the following recommendations:

5 to act consistently to uphold human beings' basic rights:

a. by agreeing principles and criteria for specific UN responses, including peacekeeping under Chapter 7 of the Charter, for civilians threatened by intra-state and inter-state conflict;

6 to strengthen the UN's ability to undertake preventive action:

a. by establishing an Office of Preventive Diplomacy, within the UN Secretariat, to collate early-warning information from governments, UN departments and agencies, non-governmental organisations, the media, and academic researchers;

b. by securing the UN Security Council's agreement to consider appropriate preventive action in response to all reports from the Office of Preventive Diplomacy presented to it by the Secretary-General;

c. by establishing UN human rights monitors, 'white helmets', available for immediate deployment on the authority of the Secretary-General;

7 to reduce the flow of arms to areas where they are likely to result in civilian suffering:

a. by declaring arms exports to the UN's Register of Conventional Arms, and extending the Register to include small arms;

b. by agreeing and enforcing a code of conduct on international arms transfers;

c. by banning the production, sale, export, transfer, stockpiling, and use of anti-personnel mines at the review of the Inhumane Weapons Convention in September 1995;

8 to improve the UN's readiness to mount peacekeeping operations:

a. by establishing better stand-by arrangements for troops, civilian police, and logistical support and equipment made available to the UN, for actions under both Chapter 6 and Chapter 7 of the Charter;[56]

b. by training troops offered under these arrangements for peacekeeping duties, with the onus falling on UN member states with the greatest military capacity and expertise;

c. by increasing the peacekeeping reserve fund to at least US$400 million;

d. by allowing the Secretary-General to oblige governments to contribute 20 per cent of the estimated costs of peacekeeping operations immediately after Security Council authorisation;

e. by fully and swiftly paying assessed contributions to the UN's peacekeeping budgets;

9 to strengthen the UN's capacity to undertake peace-keeping operations in future:

a. by establishing a UN rapid deployment force for preventive and peacekeeping duties, to be deployed following Security Council authorisation, under Chapter 6 and 7 of the UN Charter;

10 to enhance the effectiveness of the UN's humanitarian response to emergencies:

a. by conducting a public evaluation of the response of UN departments and agencies to the refugee crisis in Goma, to establish what lessons can be learned;

b. by fully and swiftly funding all UN Consolidated Appeals;

c. by ensuring that the UN Department of Humanitarian

Affairs (DHA) has the authority to co-ordinate the actions of separate UN agencies responding to an emergency;

d. by considering whether the fundamental problems of co-ordination between disparate agencies responding to an emergency should be resolved by the creation of a new UN Department, incorporating the functions of the existing agencies and DHA under a Deputy Secretary-General;

e. by ensuring that the mandate of any such new department covers people displaced within their own countries, as well as refugees.

Appendix: Oxfam's Programme in the Great Lakes Region

Oxfam (UK and Ireland) has been funding projects in Rwanda and the Great Lakes region (Tanzania, Zaire, Uganda, and Burundi) since the 1960s, and opened its own office in Kigali in 1979. During the 1980s Oxfam's work in Rwanda concentrated on encouraging the formation of Rwandese NGOs working with peasant farmers.

Since 1990, Oxfam's work has increasingly been in the form of emergency relief, although development work continued up until April 1994, and in 1992 Oxfam funded education projects on non-violence and democracy. Following the RPF invasion in 1990 and the Rwandese government's military response, hundreds of thousands of Rwandese were internally displaced, and Oxfam established a major emergency programme to help to meet their needs for urgent relief.

Another emergency programme was established to provide relief to people displaced by the fighting in the Kivu region of Zaire in 1993. Oxfam also launched a major emergency programme for the Burundese refugees who fled to southern Rwanda following the military coup in Burundi in October 1993. Over £740,000 has been spent on this programme, which delivered safe water supplies, sanitation facilities, and health care.

In response to developments in Rwanda since April 1994, Oxfam has launched one of the largest emergency operations in its 50-year history. Most of Oxfam's work has been with Rwandese refugees in neighbouring countries; but Oxfam also carried out a water and health programme for the displaced in northern Rwanda (spending over £2 million). In Tanzania, Oxfam is the lead agency supplying water to 330,000 Rwandese refugees in the Ngara district, and has a major water, health, and sanitation programme in the Karagwe district. Since April 1994, Oxfam has spent over £3,730,000 in Tanzania.

Oxfam is also working with Rwandese refugees in Burundi, providing technical assistance and water equipment in six refugee camps. In response to the refugee crisis in Goma, Zaire, Oxfam embarked upon a huge water-supply programme, and is the lead agency providing water to over 700,000 Rwandese refugees in the North Kivu region. Since July 1994, Oxfam has spent £4,439,000 on this work. Oxfam has also worked with the small number of Rwandese refugees who have fled to Uganda since April, and has plans for relief work in the Bukavu region of Zaire. To date, Oxfam has spent over £10 million on emergency relief work in the Great Lakes region since April 1994.

In support of its work in the field, Oxfam (UK and Ireland), and other members of the Oxfam family, have campaigned to raise awareness about developments in Rwanda, and lobbied governments and the UN system with specific policy proposals. In future years, Oxfam will continue its emergency work in the region, and aims to re-establish a development programme when conditions allow.

Acknowledgements

I am very grateful to all those colleagues in Oxfam (UK and Ireland) who found time, during an exceptionally busy period, to read and comment on early drafts of this book. It would be unfair to name individuals, but I particularly want to thank David Waller for his very generous contribution of time and expertise. Readers who want to know more about the background to the current crisis in the Great Lakes region, and about long-term development prospects for Rwanda, should read his book *Rwanda: Which Way Now?*, published by Oxfam (UK and Ireland) in 1993.

Guy Vassall-Adams
September 1994

Notes

1. United Nations Development Programme, *Human Development Report 1994*.

2. David Waller, *Rwanda: Which Way Now?*, Oxford: Oxfam, 1993.

3. See note 1.

4. World Bank, *World Debt Tables 1992-93*.

5. See note 1.

6. Peter Wiles, 'Rwandese Refugees and Migrants in the Great Lakes Region of Central Africa', report for Oxfam, December 1992. (Because of the lack of reliable census data in the region, all these figures are estimates and should be treated with extreme caution.)

7. Charles P. Gasarasi, 'The Mass Naturalization and Further Integration of Rwandese Refugees in Tanzania: Process, Problems and Prospects', academic paper.

8. See note 7.

9. Catharine Watson, 'Transition in Burundi', US Committee for Refugees, September 1993.

10. See note 2.

11. The Dar es Salaam Declaration on the Rwandese Refugee Problem, 19 February 1991.

12. AfricaWatch, *Talking Peace and Waging War*, 27 February 1992.

13. Amnesty International, *Persecution of Tutsi Minority and Repression of Government Critics 1990-92*, May 1992.

14. AfricaWatch, *Beyond the Rhetoric: Continuing Human Rights Abuses in Rwanda*, June 1993.

15. B.W. Ndiaye, Report to the UN Economic and Social Council, 11 August 1993.

16. Human Rights Watch Arms Project, *Arming Rwanda: The Arms Trade and Human Rights Abuses in the Rwandan War*', January 1994.

17. See note 16.

18. See note 16.

19. Economist Intelligence Unit, *Rwanda Country Report*, Fourth Quarter 1993.

20. Economist Intelligence Unit, *Rwanda Country Report*, First Quarter 1994.

21. Economist Intelligence Unit, *Rwanda Country Report*, Second Quarter 1994.

22. See note 20.

23. See note 21.

24. See note 21.

25. Dr B. Boutros-Ghali, *Report of the Secretary-General on the United Nations Assistance Mission for Rwanda*, 30 December 1993.

26. See note 21.

27. Testimony submitted to a Special Session of the UN Commission on Human Rights, 25 May 1994.

28. See note 21.

29. Dr B. Boutros-Ghali, *Report of the Secretary General on the Situation in Rwanda*, 13 May 1994.

30. Victoria Brittain, Edward Luce, 'Aid agencies condemn UN pull-out from Rwanda', *Guardian*, 23 April 1994.

31. Dr Salim Ahmed Salim, press release, Addis Ababa, 22 April 1994.

32. Catherine Bond, 'Dispatches' Channel Four TV, 1994.

33. David Orr, 'We have seen terrible things these last two weeks', *Independent*,16 May 1994'

34. 'UN fears new round of killing in Rwanda', *International Herald Tribune*, 14/15 May 1994.

35. President Ali Hassan Mwinyi, , State House speech, 1 May 1994.

36. See note 29.

37. *International Herald Tribune*, leading article, 'Shameful dawdling', 16 June 1994.

38. Richard Dowden, 'UN chief pleads for more peace-keepers', *Independent*, 8 May 1994.

39. Dr B. Boutros-Ghali, *Report of the Secretary General on the Situation in Rwanda*, 31 May 1994.

40. *The Economist*, 'The French in Rwanda', 2 July 1994.

41. *Africa Confidential*, 'Rwanda: implausible deniability', 15 July 1994.

42. See note 40.

43. Leslie Crawford, 'French save hundreds of badly wounded Tutsi', *Financial Times* ,1 July 1994.

44. Maurice Herson, Situation Report to Oxfam from Goma, 9 July 1994.

45. *Independent* and *Guardian* in London.

46. Buchizya Mseteka, 'Human tide flows over Zaire border', 14 July 1994.

47. Chris McGreal, 'Refugee death rate soars in Zaire', *Guardian*, 26 July 1994.

48. Chris McGreal, 'Beyond despair', *Guardian* 27 July 1994.

49. See note 48.

50. Nicholas Stockton, Situation Report to Oxfam from Goma, 28 July 1994.

51. Nicholas Stockton, verbal communication, Oxford, September 1994.

52. Nicholas Stockton, notes on a telephone call from Goma, 29 July 1994.

53. The UNHCR's estimate on 29 August was 46,000.

54. Lindsey Hilsum, 'RPF troops "kill Hutus on their way home"', *Guardian*, 5 August 1994.

55. America hampers dispatch of extra UN troops for Rwanda', *Independent*, 18 May 1994.

56. UN peacekeeping under Chapter 6 of the UN Charter requires the consent of the parties on the ground. UN peacekeeping under Chapter 7 does not require such consent.